The Key to the Keyboard

P A Murphy FFTCom FSCT

Head of Secretarial Studies
Fleetwood Hesketh High School and Sixth Form College

Pitman

PITMAN PUBLISHING
128 Long Acre, London, WC2E 9AN

A Division of Longman Group UK Limited

© Longman Group Limited 1983

First published in Great Britain 1983
Ninth impression 1992

ISBN 0 273 03633 5

Filmset in 10/12 V.I.P. Helvetica

Produced by Longman Singapore Publishers Pte Ltd
Printed in Singapore

Contents

Introduction

As a teacher of typewriting, I have long thought that a simple keyboard instruction book, containing ample practice exercises, was needed. The absence of such a basic textbook for beginners caused me to compile this book. It is intended to enable the students to become proficient in the use of the keyboard. The individual can then proceed, with further tuition, to the typing of letters, displays, tabulations, etc with a sound and confident knowledge of the keyboard.

This is an ideal beginners' class book for those taking Pitman and RSA courses in schools and colleges. The Teacher will find the clearly presented exercises and the regular consolidation sentences valuable in teaching young typists. Also, the short speed drills throughout are beneficial to the training of 'speed with accuracy' from the beginning.

The Key to the Keyboard can also be used by students of all ages and abilities as a self-teaching aid. The instructions can be easily followed and the pace at which the student progresses is up to the individual.

It is a useful textbook for both personal use and for those wanting 'hands on' experience for work with computers and data processing.

The typewriter and its parts

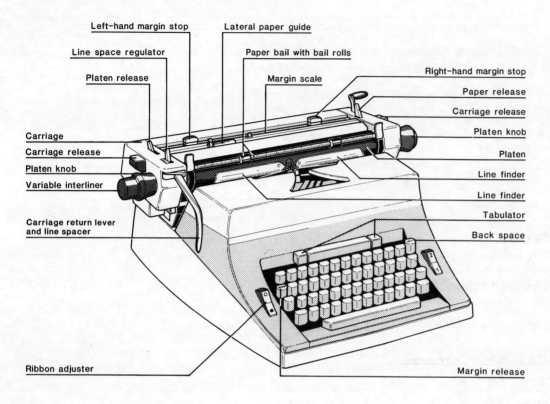

Left-hand margin stop

Line space regulator

Platen release

Carriage

Carriage release

Platen knob

Variable interliner

Carriage return lever
and line spacer

Ribbon adjuster

Lateral paper guide

Paper bail with bail rolls

Margin scale

Right-hand margin stop

Paper release

Carriage release

Platen knob

Platen

Line finder

Line finder

Tabulator

Back space

Margin release

The microcomputer

Microcomputer keyboards usually have the same layout as typewriters for the letters and punctuation marks. In addition, they have a number of special function keys. On some keyboards, the numbers are grouped together, as with a calculator, and set off to the right.

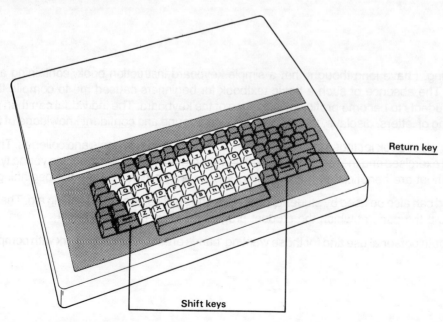

Return key

Shift keys

Home keys

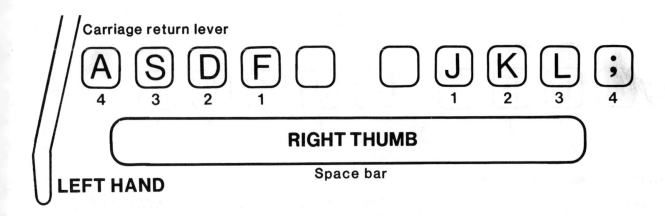

Carriage return lever

A S D F [ ] [ ] J K L ;

4 3 2 1   1 2 3 4

RIGHT THUMB

Space bar

LEFT HAND

Set margin stops throughout the book at one inch (25 mm). Scale points '12 and 88' – *Elite* **or** '10 and 72' – *Pica*.

Place your **finger tips** on the **Home Keys** with **wrists up!**

Now rest your **right thumb** lightly on the Space Bar.

Tap the Space Bar with a light quick action until you reach the right-hand side of your paper – keeping **all your fingers on the Home Keys**.

Now push the Carriage Return Lever with your left hand and as quickly as you can to the right – this will automatically turn up your paper whilst the carriage is being returned to the left-hand margin. After operating the Carriage Return Lever, make sure you return your left hand directly to the Home Keys.

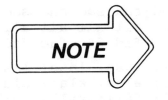

An electric typewriter has the Carriage Return Lever in the form of a Return Key, on the right-hand side of the machine, usually to the right of the Shift Key. This should be operated with the fourth finger of the right hand.

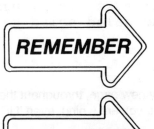

When you return the carriage with your left hand, the fingers of your right hand should **always** be resting **on the Home Keys**.

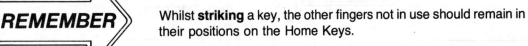

Whilst **striking** a key, the other fingers not in use should remain in their positions on the Home Keys.

 As you are approaching the end of your typing line, you will hear a 'warning bell' to indicate that only a few more letters can be typed on that line.

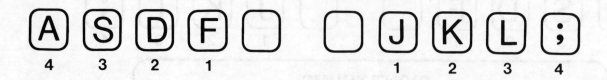

Type **one line** of **each** of the following: –

First finger left hand: –	`fffff space fffff fffff fffff fffff`
First finger right hand: –	`jjjjj space jjjjj jjjjj jjjjj jjjjj`
Second finger left hand: –	`ddddd ddddd ddddd ddddd ddddd ddddd`
Second finger right hand: –	`kkkkk kkkkk kkkkk kkkkk kkkkk kkkkk`
Third finger left hand: –	`sssss sssss sssss sssss sssss sssss`
Third finger right hand: –	`lllll lllll lllll lllll lllll lllll`
Fourth finger left hand: –	`aaaaa aaaaa aaaaa aaaaa aaaaa aaaaa`
Fourth finger right hand: –	`;;;;; ;;;;; ;;;;; ;;;;; ;;;;; ;;;;;`

Type **five lines** of the following: –

`asdf ;lkj asdf ;lkj asdf ;lkj asdf`

Type **one line** of **each** of the following words: –

```
dad dad dad dad dad dad dad dad dad
lad lad lad lad lad lad lad lad lad
sad sad sad sad sad sad sad sad sad
all all all all all all all all all
fad fad fad fad fad fad fad fad fad

lass; lass; lass; lass; lass; lass;
alas; alas; alas; alas; alas; alas;
fall; fall; fall; fall; fall; fall;
asks; asks; asks; asks; asks; asks;
salad salad salad salad salad salad
```

 Do not begin any new page, throughout the book, until you have mastered the one you are typing, even if it involves typing a page more than once.

Home keys

4   3   2   1   1   2   3   4

New letter

**First finger
LEFT HAND**

Place your fingers on your Home Keys.

First finger, left hand, moves slightly to the right to strike letter 'g' whilst the remaining fingers stay on the Home Keys. Feel the reach from 'f' to 'g' and then back to 'f'.

Type **two lines** of the following: —

```
fgf fgf fgf fgf fgf fgf fgf fgf fgf
fgf fgf fgf fgf fgf fgf fgf fgf fgf
```

Every time you strike the Space Bar, **all** your fingers should be resting on the Home Keys.

Type **one line** of **each** of the following words: —

```
sag sag sag sag sag sag sag sag sag
gas gas gas gas gas gas gas gas gas
fag fag fag fag fag fag fag fag fag
slag; slag; slag; slag; slag; slag;
flags flags flags flags flags flags
glass glass glass glass glass glass
```

Type each of the above new words alternately.

eg: —   `sag gas fag slag; flags glass`

This example applies throughout the book.

Home keys

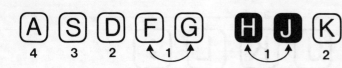

4   3   2   1   1   2   3   4

Short revision

Type two lines of: –
Type two lines of: –
Type two lines of: –

```
asdfgf asdfgf asdfgf asdfgf asdfgf
sag gas fag sag gas fag sag gas fag
glass slag; galas flags glass slag;
```

New letter  **First finger**
RIGHT HAND

Place your fingers on your Home Keys.

First finger right hand, moves slightly to the left to strike letter 'h' whilst the remaining fingers stay on the Home Keys. Feel the reach from 'j' to 'h' and then back to 'j'.

Type **two lines** of the following: –

```
jhj jhj jhj jhj jhj jhj jhj jhj jhj
jhj jhj jhj jhj jhj jhj jhj jhj jhj
```

Type **two lines** of the following: –

```
asdfgf ;lkjhj asdfgf ;lkjhj asdfgf
;lkjhj asdfgf ;lkjhj asdfgf ;lkjhj
```

Type **two lines** of the following: –

```
jaffas; jaffas; jaffas; jaffas; jaffas;
jaffas; jaffas; jaffas; jaffas; jaffas;
```

Type **one line** of **each** of the following words: –

```
has has has has has has has has has
ash ash ash ash ash ash ash ash ash
had had had had had had had had had

gash gash gash gash gash gash gash
hall hall hall hall hall hall hall
hash hash hash hash hash hash hash

shall shall shall shall shall shall
flags flags flags flags flags flags
halls halls halls halls halls halls
```

Type each of the above new words alternately as before.

Revision sentences

Type each of the following sentences **twice on each line**, putting into practice all the keys you have learned so far.

In between each of the two sentences on the one line, leave **two spaces** – tap the Space Bar **twice** instead of the usual once between words. This is to prevent the sentences running into one another.

```
a salad glass has a sad fall
a glad lass had salad
a flag had a sad fall
dad had a salad
has dad had a salad glass
dad had a fag
has dad had hash
ask dad
a lass had a sad fall
shall a lass fall
a flask had a fall
alas dad falls
a lass has a dad
a lad has a dad
dad has a flask
has dad had a flask
```

If you can type the first two sentences **twice** in one minute, you are typing at a speed of 20 words per minute (wpm).

If, however, you make any errors, these should be deducted from the 20 wpm. For example, if you have three errors, this means that you can type ACCURATELY at 17 wpm.

New letter

LEFT HAND

Second finger left hand reaches **up to the left** to strike the letter 'e'. First, feel the reach from 'd' to 'e' and then back to 'd'.

Type **two lines** of the following: –

```
ded ded ded ded ded ded ded ded ded
ded ded ded ded ded ded ded ded ded
```

REMEMBER

Keep your **wrists up** in order to allow your fingers to each for the keys on the row above.

The fingers not in use should always be resting **lightly** on the Home Keys.

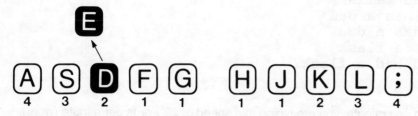

Type **one line** of **each** of the following words: –

```
deal deal deal deal deal deal deal
seed seed seed seed seed seed seed
fled fled fled fled fled fled fled
sage sage sage sage sage sage sage

feels feels feels feels feels feels
seals seals seals seals seals seals
lease lease lease lease lease lease
heels heels heels heels heels heels
```

Type each of the following sentences **twice** on **each line**: –

```
ask dad has he a lease
she shall fall
he feels he shall fall
he has aged
she has a lead
she seals dads flask
dad feels sad
he heals a sad lass
she seeks a seal
```

New letter

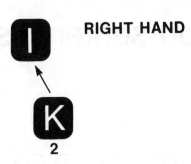

RIGHT HAND

Second finger right hand reaches **up to the left** to strike the letter 'i'. First, feel the reach from 'k' to 'i' and then back to 'k'.

Type **two lines** of the following: –

```
kik kik kik kik kik kik kik kik kik
```

Keep your wrists up.

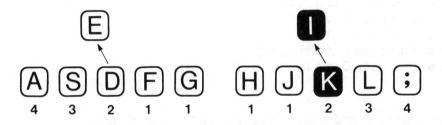

A	S	D	F	G		H	J	K	L	;
4	3	2	1	1		1	1	2	3	4

Type **one line** of **each** of the following words: –

```
hid hid hid hid hid hid hid hid hid
lid lid lid lid lid lid lid lid lid
ill ill ill ill ill ill ill ill ill
his his his his his his his his his

kill kill kill kill kill kill kill
kiss kiss kiss kiss kiss kiss kiss
aids aids aids aids aids aids aids
silk silk silk silk silk silk silk
lies lies lies lies lies lies lies
dies dies dies dies dies dies dies

sides sides sides sides sides sides
likes likes likes likes likes likes
aided aided aided aided aided aided
liked liked liked liked liked liked
aside aside aside aside aside aside
glide glide glide glide glide glide
```

Type each of the above words alternately.

Revision sentences

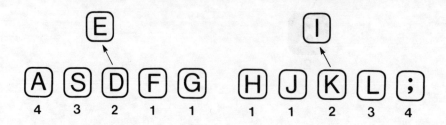

Type each of the following sentences **twice** on **each** line, putting into practice all the keys you have learned so far.

```
he is a deaf lad
she is a deaf lass
he lashes his side
he lies ill alas
she is ill
he has aged
she has died
he aids his dad
he has killed his dad
she has all his slides
he is like his dad
she has a silk flag
his aged dad is liked
his dad died alas
```

If you can type the first seven sentences **once** in one minute, you are typing at 20 wpm.

New letter

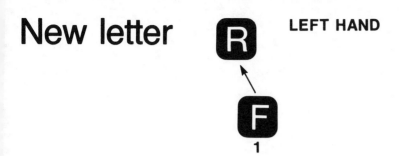

LEFT HAND

First finger left hand reaches **up** to the **left** to strike the letter 'r'. First, feel the reach from 'f' to 'r' and then back to 'f'.

Type **two lines** of the following: –

```
frf frf frf frf frf frf frf frf
frf frf frf frf frf frf frf frf
```

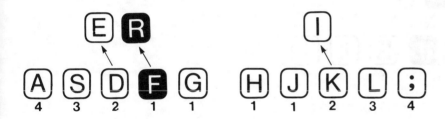

Type **one line** of **each** of the following words: –

```
red red red red red red red red
led led led led led led led led
her her her her her her her her

fear fear fear fear fear fear fear
ride ride ride ride ride ride ride
here here here here here here here
sire sire sire sire sire sire sire
hear hear hear hear hear hear hear
hire hire hire hire hire hire hire
liar liar liar liar liar liar liar
rash rash rash rash rash rash rash
rigs rigs rigs rigs rigs rigs rigs

dress dress dress dress dress dress
reads reads reads reads reads reads
fears fears fears fears fears fears
fires fires fires fires fires fires
fried fried fried fried fried fried

desire desire desire desire desire
raided raided raided raided raided
flared flared flared flared flared
```

Type each of the above words alternately.

13

New letter

RIGHT HAND

First finger right hand reaches **up** to the **left** to strike the letter 'u'. Feel the reach from 'j' to 'u' and then back to 'j'.

Type **two lines** of the following: –

```
juj juj juj juj juj juj juj juj juj
juj juj juj juj juj juj juj juj juj
```

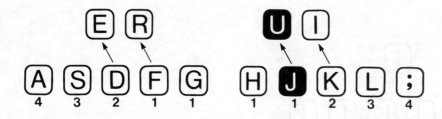

Type **one line** of **each** of the following words: –

```
due due due due due due due due due
fur fur fur fur fur fur fur fur fur
hug hug hug hug hug hug hug hug hug
sue sue sue sue sue sue sue sue sue

drug drug drug drug drug drug drug
user user user user user user user
full full full full full full full
jugs jugs jugs jugs jugs jugs jugs
suds suds suds suds suds suds suds

sugar sugar sugar sugar sugar sugar
sulks sulks sulks sulks sulks sulks
suede suede suede suede suede suede

rulers rulers rulers rulers rulers
duffle duffle duffle duffle duffle
argues argues argues argues argues
rugged rugged rugged rugged rugged
frugal frugal frugal frugal frugal
drudge drudge drudge drudge drudge
```

Type each of the above words alternately.

Revision sentences

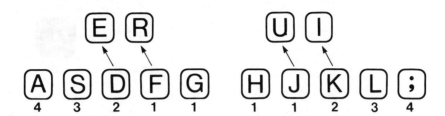

Type each of the following sentences **twice** on **each** line, putting into practice all the keys you have learned so far.

```
a dull silk dress
she has red heels
she hears his lies
he is sure his eggs fell
shell her eggs dad
he hears a seagull
he likes his sugar
she has a full jug
he has a red ruler
dad has a faded duffle
he has drugs alas
she has real red hair
dad likes his red fire
he hired a glass hall
```

If you can type the first three sentences **twice** in one minute, you are typing at 20 wpm.

Introduction of the Full Stop

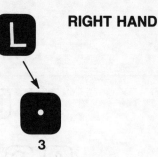

The third finger of the right hand reaches **down** to the **right** for the 'Full Stop'. Keep your **wrists up** in order to allow your fingers to reach the bottom row of keys. Practice the reach from letter 'l' down to the 'Full Stop'. **Strike the full stop lightly** in order that a deep impression is avoided in the paper.

l.l l.l l.l l.l l.l l.l l.l l.l
l.l l.l l.l l.l l.l l.l l.l l.l

When using the full stop – at the **end of a sentence only** – make sure you depress the Space Bar **twice** after the full stop.

You must always leave **two spaces** between each sentence.

Type, **twice** on each line, the first six revision sentences on the previous page, inserting a full stop at the end of each sentence.

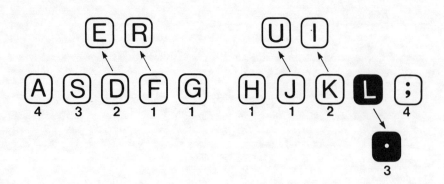

Introduction of the Shift Keys

LEFT HAND   **RIGHT HAND**

Shift Keys are used to make capital letters. These keys are struck by the fourth finger of the left **or** right hand. The Shift Key must be held down firmly until the letter required has been struck and allowed to return to the key basket. Therefore make sure your first finger of each hand is always resting on the Home Key of either 'f' or 'j' whilst reaching down for the Shift Keys.

If you require a capital letter with a finger from the left hand – as in 'Dad' – the **right Shift Key** is held down with the fourth finger of the right hand, whilst the letter 'D' is struck with the second finger of the left hand. If 'High Hill' is required, then the **left Shift Key** will be used, whilst the letter 'H' is struck with the first finger of the right hand.

Type **one line** of **each** of the following words: –

```
Dad Dad Dad Dad Dad Dad Dad Dad
He He He He He He He He He He
She She She She She She She She
```

Type the following, remembering to leave **two** spaces after the full stop: –

```
Sal.  Fred.  Sal.  Fred.  Sal.
Dear.  Sir.  Dear.  Sir.  Dear.
```

The Shift Lock, which is above the Shift Key, will, when depressed, enable you to type in ALL CAPITAL LETTERS. To release, press the Shift Key.

New letter

Third finger left hand reaches **up** to the **left** to strike the letter 'w'. First, feel the reach from 's' up to 'w' and then back to 's'.

Type **two lines** of the following: –

```
sws  sws  sws  sws  sws  sws  sws  sws
sws  sws  sws  sws  sws  sws  sws  sws
```

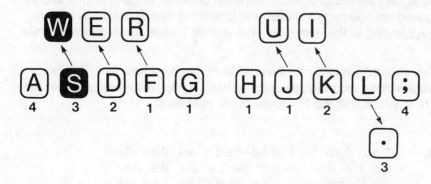

Type **one line** of **each** of the following words: –

```
saw saw saw saw saw saw saw saw
was was was was was was was was
awe awe awe awe awe awe awe awe
law law law law law law law law
raw raw raw raw raw raw raw raw
few few few few few few few few

wise wise wise wise wise wise wise
draw draw draw draw draw draw draw
wash wash wash wash wash wash wash
flaw flaw flaw flaw flaw flaw flaw
grew grew grew grew grew grew grew

sewer sewer sewer sewer sewer sewer
wedge wedge wedge wedge wedge wedge
fewer fewer fewer fewer fewer fewer
wells wells wells wells wells wells

walker walker walker walker walker
swears swears swears swears swears
wiggle wiggle wiggle wiggle wiggle
wishes wishes wishes wishes wishes
swedes swedes swedes swedes swedes
drawer drawer drawer drawer drawer
```

Type each of the above words alternately, inserting a Capital Letter at the beginning of each word. eg:

```
Saw Was Awe Law Raw Few Wise Draw
Wash Flaw Grew Sewer Wedge Fewer
Wells Walker Swears Wiggle Wishes
Swedes Drawer
```

Revision sentences

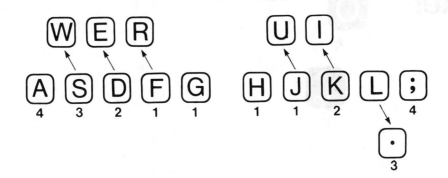

New listening instructions/skills

The typing of the sentences twice on one line in this and the following exercises, may not always be possible. You must train yourself to listen for the warning bell on your typewriter, which will ring as you are approaching the end of your typing line, because of the right-hand margin stop which you have set.

Complete the word which you are typing, but do not start to type a new word. Finish typing the remainder of the second sentence on the next line.

Begin each group of two sentences on a new line.

Type each of the following sentences **twice** on **each** line (where possible) putting into practice all the keys you have learned so far.

```
She washes her dishes.
He wishes she was wiser.
She saw her dress was dull.
She sews her dresses herself.
Her drawers are wide.
Dad swears like Fred.
Fred grew his hair.
Dad said she was well.
Fred likes a high fell walk.
Jill was a sad girl.
A few girls are well liked.
Ida has fair hair as well as Dad.
Sarah fried her eggs.
Sue likes Sarah.
A dwarf is well liked.
```

If you can type the first four sentences **once** in one minute, you are typing at 20 wpm.

New letter

RIGHT HAND

Third finger right hand reaches **up** to the **left** to strike the letter 'o'. First, feel the reach from 'l' to 'o' and then back to 'l'.

Type **two lines** of the following: –

```
lol lol lol lol lol lol lol lol lol
lol lol lol lol lol lol lol lol lol
```

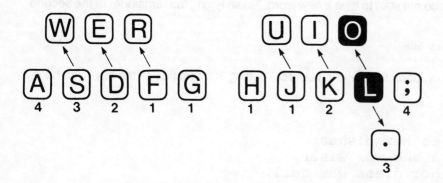

Type **one line** of **each** of the following words: –

```
owl owl owl owl owl owl owl owl owl
low low low low low low low low low
how how how how how how how how how
sow sow sow sow sow sow sow sow sow
oil oil oil oil oil oil oil oil oil

grow grow grow grow grow grow grow
hole hole hole hole hole hole hole
look look look look look look look
food food food food food food food
slow slow slow slow slow slow slow
roof roof roof roof roof roof roof

slower slower slower slower slower
grower grower grower grower grower
hooked hooked hooked hooked hooked
worker worker worker worker worker
wooded wooded wooded wooded wooded
flower flower flower flower flower
shower shower shower shower shower
holder holder holder holder holder

foolish foolish foolish foolish
goulash goulash goulash goulash
```

Type each of the above words alternately.

Introduction of the Question Mark

The question mark ('?') can be found at the right-hand side of the typewriter and can be obtained by holding the left Shift Key down, whilst striking the '?' key. Use the fourth finger left hand for the Shift Key and fourth finger right hand for the question mark.

The Question Mark Key varies its position on the typewriter, according to the make of machine, but it is always struck by the fourth finger of the right hand.

Type **two lines** of the following: –

```
;?;  ;?;  ;?;  ;?;  ;?;  ;?;  ;?;
;?;  ;?;  ;?;  ;?;  ;?;  ;?;  ;?;
```

The question mark acts as a full stop, therefore **two** spaces are required after it.

Type each of the following sentences **twice** on **each** line.

```
Is her owl good?
Does she swear aloud?
Where is her dog?
How is she dressed?
Has she had a shower?
Who is he like?
```

Revision sentences

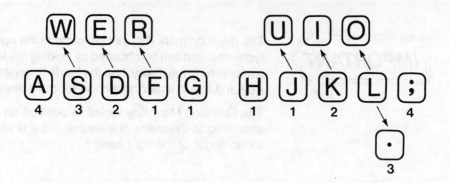

Type each of the following sentences **twice** on **each** line, putting into practice all the keys you have learned so far.

```
Who grows food?
She grows food.
He feels low.
Draw a row of houses.
His hood is of wool.
He likes his fowl.
We were housed afar.
His wheel is slow.
She swears aloud.
He has a shower.
Her owl is as good as gold.
She is a good walker.
Work hard for good rewards.
Where are our dresses?
Who was here for a week?
Her hair was like wool.
Dad sold his wireless alas.
```

If you can type the first six sentences **once** in one minute, you are typing at 20 wpm.

New letter

LEFT HAND

First finger left hand reaches **up to the right** for the letter 't'.

This is the **only** letter reach on the top row of keys which goes **up** to the **right** – all the other letter reaches go **up** to the **left**. Feel the reach first from 'f' up to 't' and back to 'f'.

Type **two lines** of the following: –

```
ftf ftf ftf ftf ftf ftf ftf ftf ftf
ftf ftf ftf ftf ftf ftf ftf ftf ftf
```

Type **two lines** of the following: –

```
frftf frftf frftf frftf frftf frftf
frftf frftf frftf frftf frftf frftf
```

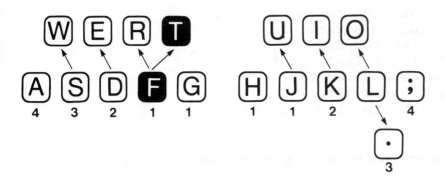

Type **one line** of **each** of the following words: –

```
hit hit hit hit hit hit hit hit hit
got got got got got got got got got
let let let let let let let let let
tar tar tar tar tar tar tar tar tar
rat rat rat rat rat rat rat rat rat

seat seat seat seat seat seat seat
tear tear tear tear tear tear tear
that that that that that that that
what what what what what what what

faith faith faith faith faith faith
light light light light light light
treat treat treat treat treat treat
greet greet greet greet greet greet
heart heart heart heart heart heart
tiger tiger tiger tiger tiger tiger
sweet sweet sweet sweet sweet sweet
drift drift drift drift drift drift
```

Type each of the above words alternately.

Revision sentences

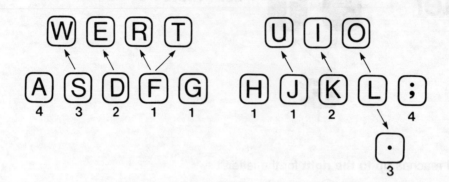

Type each of the following sentences **twice** on **each** line, putting into practice all the keys you have learned so far.

```
Walk towards the wall.
Work hard for good results.
The roof has two holes.
The tiger was tearful.
He was there to greet her.
He let the tar set.
She had a sweet tooth.
She drifted towards earth.
What was her hat treated with?
The girl ate the tarts herself.
It is right to agree.
Heat the fat for Dad.
Where is their flat sheet?
Her heart was tired out.
The tiger was swift.
It was right to light the fire.
```

If you can type the first five sentences **once** in one minute, you are typing at 24 wpm.

New letter

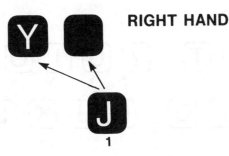

RIGHT HAND

First finger right hand reaches **up** to the **left** to strike the letter 'y'.

NOTE

This is an extra long reach because the first finger of the right hand also reaches up to the left for the letter 'u'.

Feel the reach from 'j' to 'y' and back to 'j'.

Type **two lines** of the following: –

```
jyj jyj jyj jyj jyj jyj jyj jyj jyj
jyj jyj jyj jyj jyj jyj jyj jyj jyj
```

Type **two lines** of the following: –

```
jujyj jujyj jujyj jujyj jujyj jujyj
jujyj jujyj jujyj jujyj jujyj jujyj
```

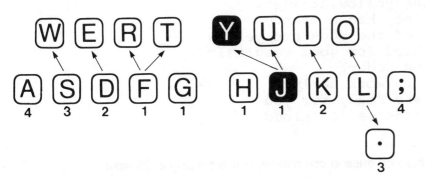

Type **one line** of **each** of the following words: –

```
yes yes yes yes yes yes yes yes yes
yet yet yet yet yet yet yet yet yet
hay hay hay hay hay hay hay hay hay
say say say say say say say say say

yolk yolk yolk yolk yolk yolk yolk
yoga yoga yoga yoga yoga yoga yoga
tray tray tray tray tray tray tray
they they they they they they they
yell yell yell yell yell yell yell
your your your your your your your

yield yield yield yield yield yield
yeast yeast yeast yeast yeast yeast
youth youth youth youth youth youth

yellow yellow yellow yellow yellow
lastly lastly lastly lastly lastly

Yorkshire Yorkshire Yorkshire
yesterday yesterday yesterday
```

Type each of the above words alternately.

Revision sentences

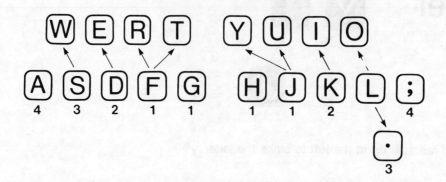

Type each of the following sentences **twice** on **each** line, putting into practice all the keys you have learned so far.

```
They all yelled at her.
She said she had to hurry.
Harry had a treat today.
They had a great day today.
Terry tried to fly freely.
Try to wait for your sister.
The youth yielded at karate.
The hay was yellow at last.
They say they had a tray.
The yolks of the eggs are yellow.
You work hard for good results.
How are you today?
Always go to work early.
Yes they are ready for you.
The yoga lads yelled aloud.
```

If you can type the first five sentences **once** in one minute, you are typing at 25 wpm.

New letter

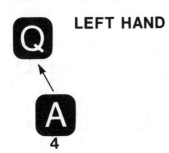

LEFT HAND

Fourth finger left hand reaches **up** to the **left** to strike the letter 'q'. Feel the reach from 'a' to 'q' and then back to 'a'. Keep your **wrists up** to allow free movement of fingers.

Type **two lines** of the following: –

```
aqa aqa aqa aqa aqa aqa aqa aqa aqa
aqa aqa aqa aqa aqa aqa aqa aqa aqa
```

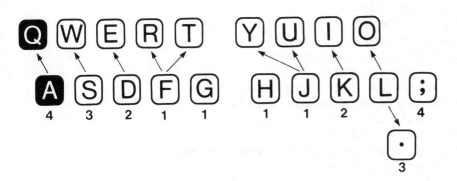

Type **one line** of **each** of the following words: –

```
queue queue queue queue queue queue
query query query query query query
quote quote quote quote quote quote
queer queer queer queer queer queer
quite quite quite quite quite quite

square square square square square
squash squash squash squash squash
squeal squeal squeal squeal squeal
quarry quarry quarry quarry quarry
quarto quarto quarto quarto quarto

quarrel quarrel quarrel quarrel
queried queried queried queried
quality quality quality quality
quarter quarter quarter quarter
```

Type each of the above words alternately.

27

Revision sentences

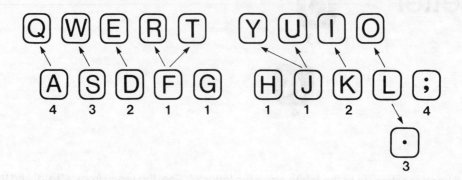

Type each of the following sentences **twice** on **each** line, putting into practice all the keys you have learned so far.

```
Dad had a quarrel at the quarry.
The hall was square.
Lisa likes her squash.
Sarah quoted what was said.
The rat squealed aloud.
The quality of the quartet was good.
It was a queer way to go away.
He weighed a quarter of sweets.
The queue was quite quiet.
Sally had a liqueur after her tea.
The toffee had quite a queer taste.
Larry had a quarrel with Dorothy.
Dad quit his work today.
The squatter stayed at the square house.
The girl quoted her story.
The safety of the quarry was queried.
```

If you can type the first five sentences **once** in one minute, you are typing at 25 wpm.

New letter

RIGHT HAND

Fourth finger right hand reaches **up** to the **left** to strike the letter 'p'. First feel the reach from ';' to 'p' and then back to ';'.

Type **two lines** of the following: –

```
;p; ;p; ;p; ;p; ;p; ;p; ;p; ;p; ;p;
;p; ;p; ;p; ;p; ;p; ;p; ;p; ;p; ;p;
```

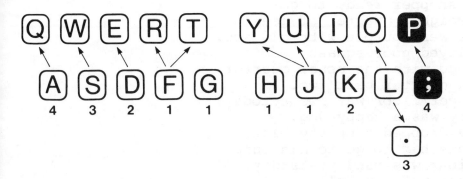

Type **one line** of **each** of the following words: –

```
pop pop pop pop pop pop pop pop pop
pat pat pat pat pat pat pat pat pat
lip lip lip lip lip lip lip lip lip
pal pal pal pal pal pal pal pal pal
pip pip pip pip pip pip pip pip pip

flap flap flap flap flap flap flap
drop drop drop drop drop drop drop
quip quip quip quip quip quip quip
part part part part part part part

purge purge purge purge purge purge
plate plate plate plate plate plate
happy happy happy happy happy happy
poppy poppy poppy poppy poppy poppy
paper paper paper paper paper paper

prefer prefer prefer prefer prefer
player player player player player
sloppy sloppy sloppy sloppy sloppy

sweeper sweeper sweeper sweeper sweeper
wrapper wrapper wrapper wrapper wrapper
parquet parquet parquet parquet parquet
shopper shopper shopper shopper shopper
platter platter platter platter platter
shipped shipped shipped shipped shipped
```

Type each of the above words alternately.

Revision sentences

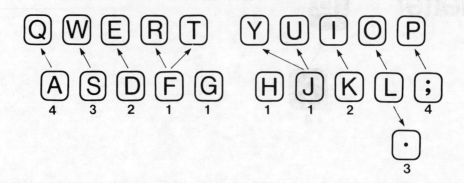

Type each of the following sentences **twice** on **each** line, putting into practice all the keys you have learned so far.

```
Paul paid for his squash.
Was the shopper ready to go?
Please weigh a quarter of peas.
His lips were purple with old age.
Peter played poor squash.
Pat played with the usual quartet.
It was a quarter past two.
The parquet floor was swept today.
The puppy was a happy dog.
The lady dropped a pretty plate.
The pirate had to go to his ship.
The parlour was used yesterday.
The pepper pot was full up.
Poppies were sold at work today.
Paul preferred to play with Fred.
The daily paper is read at our house.
The apple had large pips.
```

If you can type the first five sentences **once** in one minute, you are typing at 25 wpm.

New letter

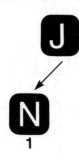

RIGHT HAND

First finger right hand is resting on the letter 'j' of the Home Keys. Reach **down** to the **left** for the letter 'n'. Just feel the reach first, keeping your wrists up to allow your fingers to reach the bottom row of keys with ease.

This is the only letter reach on the bottom row of keys which goes **down** to the **left**. All the other reaches go **down** to the **right**.

Type **two lines** of the following: –

```
jnj jnj jnj jnj jnj jnj jnj jnj
jnj jnj jnj jnj jnj jnj jnj jnj
```

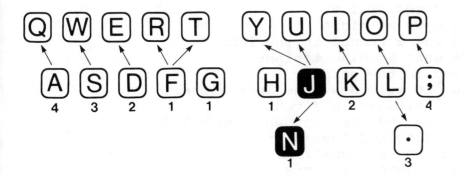

Type **one line** of **each** of the following words: –

```
ten ten ten ten ten ten ten ten
not not not not not not not not
tan tan tan tan tan tan tan tan
ton ton ton ton ton ton ton ton

nine nine nine nine nine nine
tent tent tent tent tent tent
land land land land land land
hens hens hens hens hens hens
sand sand sand sand sand sand

night night night night night
leans leans leans leans leans
plans plans plans plans plans
queen queen queen queen queen

answer answer answer answer answer
wrongs wrongs wrongs wrongs wrongs
Nellie Nellie Nellie Nellie Nellie
needle needle needle needle needle
notion notion notion notion notion
```

Type each of the above words alternately.

Revision sentences

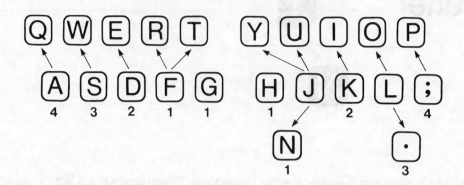

Type each of the following sentences **twice** on **each** line, putting into practice all the keys you have learned so far.

```
Linda was a happy person.
Penelope was her good friend.
Lisa went shopping late at night.
Nigel went out at noon.
She was wrong with her answer.
The plans were passed at last.
Hens lays their eggs at night.
The naughty lad dug a tunnel in the lawn.
The nightingale sang at nine tonight.
Her nephew played in the garden.
It was dangerous to walk down the lane alone.
They spent their holidays in a tent.
Norah liked the sun and the sand when on holiday.
She opened the window and leaned out.
No was the answer to the question.
Nanny knitted at nights for Linda.
Nothing happened to the naughty lad.
```

If you can type the first five lines **once** in one minute, you are typing at 28 wpm.

Type the *Revision Sentences* from the previous page before attempting to begin the New Reach on this page.

New letter

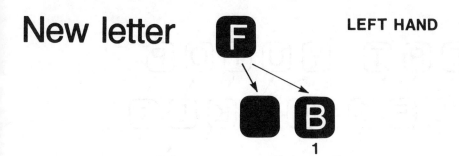

LEFT HAND

All the new reaches will now be **down** to the **right**. First finger left hand reaches from 'f' **down** to the **right** for the letter 'b'. This is an extra long reach so keep your **wrists up**. Feel the reach from 'f' to 'b' and then back to 'f'.

Type **two lines** of the following: —

```
fbf fbf fbf fbf fbf fbf fbf fbf
fbf fbf fbf fbf fbf fbf fbf fbf
```

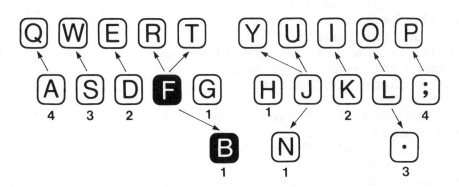

Type **one line** of **each** of the following words: —

```
bat bat bat bat bat bat bat bat
tab tab tab tab tab tab tab tab
lob lob lob lob lob lob lob lob
rob rob rob rob rob rob rob rob
web web web web web web web web

bolt bolt bolt bolt bolt bolt bolt
bare bare bare bare bare bare bare
belt belt belt belt belt belt belt
babe babe babe babe babe babe babe
knob knob knob knob knob knob knob

bobble bobble bobble bobble bobble
brands brands brands brands brands
brings brings brings brings brings
nibble nibble nibble nibble nibble
labour labour labour labour labour
baffle baffle baffle baffle baffle

blanket blanket blanket blanket
blended blended blended blended
bananas bananas bananas bananas
```

Type each of the above words alternately.

Revision sentences

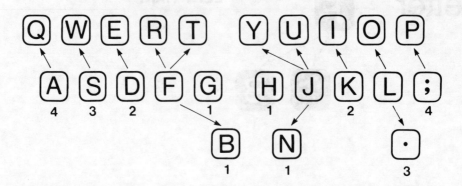

Type each of the following sentences **twice** on **each** line putting into practice all the keys you have learned so far.

```
Bring Bob the dustbin.
Brenda has brittle nails.
Barbara needs to train nightly.
The birds eat nuts in the garden.
Robin robbed the bank one night.
All things bright and beautiful.
To be or not to be that is the question.
Nine blue birds went away to be sold.
Brown is a dark shade for Belinda.
Hens lay brown eggs.
There are three bends in the lane.
Betty broke the brown bottle.
The blanket was blown off the washing line.
The parquet floor was brown.
Betty was a wonderful blind person.
Brian was her husband.
Penelope sent Belinda for her shopping.
Nigel went out at noon to bring the tent.
```

If you can type the first four sentences **once** in one minute, you are typing at 22 wpm.

New letter F → V   **LEFT HAND**

First finger left hand is resting on the letter 'f'. Reach **down** to the **right** for the letter 'v'. Feel the reach from 'f' to 'v' and then back to 'f'. The reach is not as far as from 'f' to 'b' – so be careful.

Type two lines of the following: –

```
fvf fvf fvf fvf fvf fvf fvf fvf fvf
fvf fvf fvf fvf fvf fvf fvf fvf fvf
```

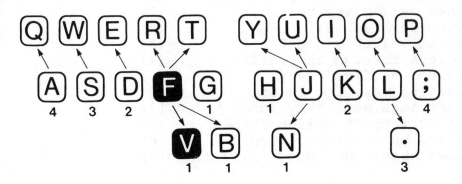

Type one line of each of the following words: –

```
vets vets vets vets vets vets vets
save save save save save save save
veil veil veil veil veil veil veil
vein vein vein vein vein vein vein
live live live live live live live
very very very very very very very

heavy heavy heavy heavy heavy heavy
slave slave slave slave slave slave
drive drive drive drive drive drive
above above above above above above
never never never never never never
valve valve valve valve valve valve

velvets velvets velvets velvets
vibrate vibrate vibrate vibrate
bravery bravery bravery bravery
variety variety variety variety
```

Type each of the above words alternately.

Revision sentences

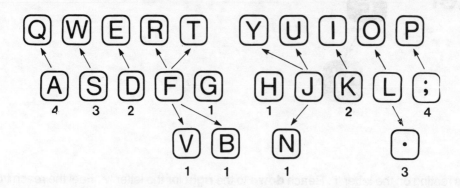

Type each of the following sentences **twice** on **each** line, putting into practice all the keys you have learned so far.

```
Valerie vowed never to tell anybody.        (7)
The affair was over very soon.              (6)
The slaves were driven through the valley.  (8)
Five brave people were saved by the dog.    (8)
Verone had a new veil given to her.         (7)
The sky was very dark above.                (6)
Have you seen the velvet gloves?            (6)
Five lorries drove through the valley.      (7)
The valve vanished at five today.           (6)
The bank valued the vase for Valerie        (7)
The veins on her legs were very sore.       (7)
The shop had a variety of velvet drapes.    (8)
The engine of the bus vibrated loudly.      (6)
Bill never drove above the speed allowed.   (8)
```

Time yourself for one minute to see how many sentences you can type. To find the number of words per minute, count up the numbers in the brackets at the end of each sentence. For example, three lines = 21 wpm.

In calculating the number of words per minute typed, the number in the bracket at the end of each line has been arrived at by averaging five strokes (including the space between words) to one word. For example, there are actually only seven typewritten words on line three, but these words differ in length and actually contain 40 strokes (including the spaces between the words) which means that when the 40 is divided by five strokes, the figure of 8 wpm is arrived at.

If the number of strokes is not divisible by five equally, then the nearest figure above has been allowed in most cases. If you are in the middle of a line when your timing is up, you count the number of strokes you have typed on that line and then divide the answer by five. This number of words is then added to the number of words in brackets at the end of the previous line, which will then give you a true answer to the speed you are typing.

New letter

RIGHT HAND

First finger right hand is resting on the letter 'j'. Reach **down** to the **right** for the letter 'm'. Feel the reach from 'j' to 'm' and then back to 'j'.

Type **two lines** of the following: –

```
jmj jmj jmj jmj jmj jmj jmj jmj jmj
jum jum jum jum jum jum jum jum jum
```

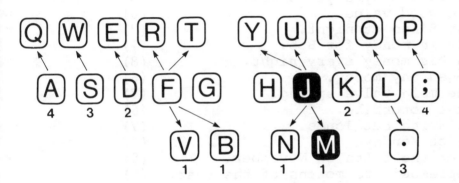

Type **one line** of **each** of the following words: –

```
hem hem hem hem hem hem hem hem hem
mid mid mid mid mid mid mid mid mid
dim dim dim dim dim dim dim dim dim
Jim Jim Jim Jim Jim Jim Jim Jim Jim
men men men men men men men men men

meal meal meal meal meal meal meal
mole mole mole mole mole mole mole
lamb lamb lamb lamb lamb lamb lamb
home home home home home home home
tomb tomb tomb tomb tomb tomb tomb

mauve mauve mauve mauve mauve mauve
money money money money money money
might might might might might might

vampire vampire vampire vampire
bombers bombers bombers bombers
monthly monthly monthly monthly
minutes minutes minutes minutes

November November November November
Vivienne Vivienne Vivienne Vivienne
```

Type each of the above words alternately.

Revision sentences

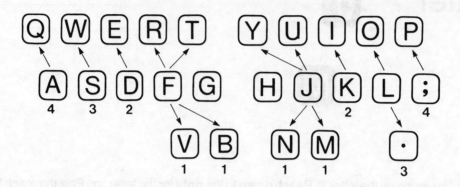

Type each of the following sentences **twice** on **each** line, putting into practice all the keys you have learned so far.

```
        Brave men vanish during wars.            (6)
        Bring Vivienne home early tonight.       (7)
        The valve broke on the tyre yesterday.   (8)
        Many bananas are good value.             (6)
        Many people play Bingo at night.         (7)
        Save five pounds in money for Bob.       (7)
        Benjamin banked his money every night.   (8)
        Brian never needed any money.            (6)
        Amanda broke the main valve spring.      (7)
        Brian has a mauve motorbike.             (6)
        His name is not Smith but Jones.         (7)
        Valerie is five on Monday.               (6)
        Remember remember the fifth of November. (8)
        November and September are months of the year. (9)
```

Check your speed. See how many sentences you can complete in one minute. To find the number of words per minute you are typing, count up the numbers in brackets at the end of each sentence.

New letter

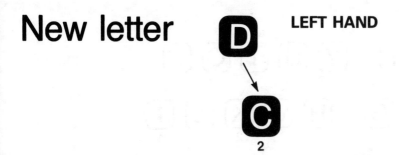

LEFT HAND

Second finger of the left hand is resting on the letter 'd'. Reach **down** to the **right** for the letter 'c'. Feel the reach first from 'd' to 'c' and then back to 'd'. Keep your **wrists up** to allow your finger to reach the bottom row of keys.

Type **two lines** of the following: –

```
dcd dcd dcd dcd dcd dcd dcd dcd dcd
dec dec dec dec dec dec dec dec dec
```

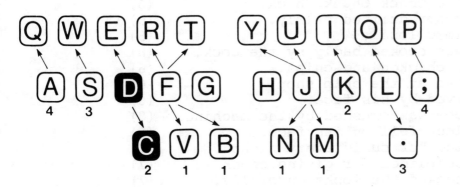

Type **one line** of **each** of the following words: –

```
cliff cliff cliff cliff cliff cliff
check check check check check check
click click click click click click
chats chats chats chats chats chats
aches aches aches aches aches aches
black black black black black black
caves caves caves caves caves caves

cobbles cobbles cobbles cobbles
combine combine combine combine
cabinet cabinet cabinet cabinet
cruiser cruiser cruiser cruiser
blanche blanche blanche blanche
becomes becomes becomes becomes
combing combing combing combing
achieve achieve achieve achieve
Charlie Charlie Charlie Charlie
deceive deceive deceive deceive
correct correct correct correct
```

Type each of the above words alternately.

Revision sentences

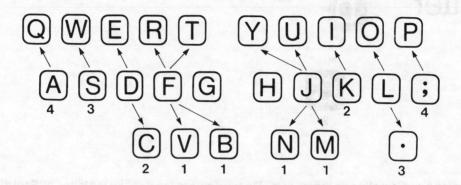

Type each of the following sentences **twice** on **each** line, putting into practice all the keys you have learned so far.

```
Come to the caves and bring the coconuts.      (8)
Carry the cotton bobbins to the office.        (8)
The Chief chatted calmly to his men.           (7)
Clumsy Clara climbed the cliffs.               (6)
Charlie Charlie Chuck Chuck Chuck.             (6)
The cabin cruiser drifted calmly.              (6)
The clock chimed loudly.                       (5)
The chicken was cooked badly by the cook.      (8)
Children love chicken and chips.               (6)
A vacancy arose at the chip shop.              (6)
She was deceived by his face.                  (6)
The cheap cocoa was crushed by the machine.    (8)
The cuckoo clock fell on its face.             (6)
The girl combed her curls every night.         (7)
Clive was disciplined for giving cheek.        (7)
The jailor checked the locks carefully.        (7)
```

Have you checked your speed? How many words per minute can you type now?

New letter

LEFT HAND

Third finger of the left hand is resting on the letter 's'. Reach **down** to the **right** for the letter 'x'. Feel the reach first from 's' to 'x' and then back to 's'. Keep your **wrists up** to allow your finger to reach the bottom key.

Type **two lines** of the following; —

```
sxs sxs sxs sxs sxs sxs sxs sxs sxs
swx swx swx swx swx swx swx swx swx
```

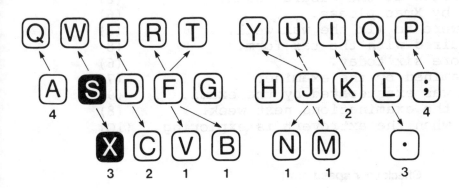

Type **one line** of **each** of the following words: —

```
tax tax tax tax tax tax tax tax tax
mix mix mix mix mix mix mix mix mix
box box box box box box box box box
wax wax wax wax wax wax wax wax wax

sixes sixes sixes sixes sixes sixes
taxis taxis taxis taxis taxis taxis
mixer mixer mixer mixer mixer mixer

extras extras extras extras extras
exhort exhort exhort exhort exhort
expect expect expect expect expect

exclaim exclaim exclaim exclaim exclaim
extract extract extract extract extract
explain explain explain explain explain

exercise exercise exercise exercise
excavate excavate excavate excavate
exported exported exported exported
exhibits exhibits exhibits exhibits
```

Type each of the above words alternately.

Revision sentences

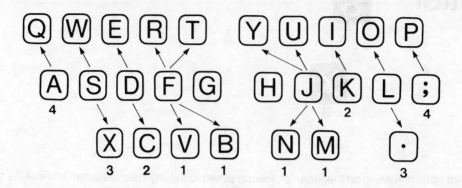

Type each of the following sentences **twice** on **each** line, where possible, putting into practice all the keys you have learned so far.

```
He explained that he was sixty years of age.      (9)
The girls exhibited their paintings as expected.   (9)
The dancing was exotic at the Cabaret Club.        (8)
Fix the xylophone by Xmas please.                  (6)
The instructions were to mix the wax well.         (8)
Extra help is required with the tax form.          (8)
Fix the boxes before six today.                    (6)
His exams were examined by the examiner.           (7)
She exclaimed she was exasperated by the exams.    (9)
He is exempt from the examinations next week.      (8)
Take extreme care when the extrovert is exploring. (10)
```

Check your speed now!

New letter

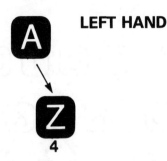

LEFT HAND

Fourth finger of the left hand is resting on the letter 'a'. Reach **down** to the **right** for the letter 'z'. Keep your **wrists up** to allow your fourth finger to reach easily for this key.

Type **two lines** of the following: –

```
aza aza aza aza aza aza aza aza aza
aqz aqz aqz aqz aqz aqz aqz aqz aqz
```

New reach

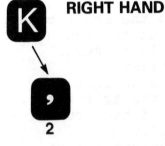

RIGHT HAND

The 'comma' is struck with the second finger of the right hand and this reach is also **down** to the **right**.

Type **two lines** of the following: –

```
k,k k,k k,k k,k k,k k,k k,k k,k k,k
ki, ki, ki, ki, ki, ki, ki, ki, ki,
```

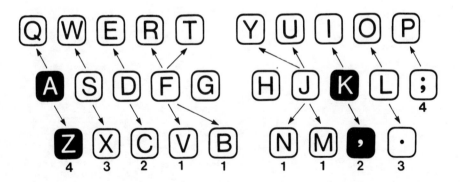

Type **one line** of **each** of the following words: –

```
zips,zips,zips,zips,zips,zips,zips,
fizz, fizz, fizz, fizz, fizz, fizz,
zero, zero, zero, zero, zero, zero,
```

```
amaze, amaze, amaze, amaze, amaze,
craze, craze, craze, craze, craze,
zebra, zebra, zebra, zebra, zebra,
pizza, pizza, pizza, pizza, pizza,
```

Type each of the above words alternately.

```
zealous, zealous, zealous, zealous,
```

43

Revision sentences

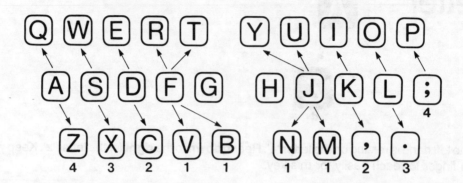

Type each of the following sentences **twice** on **each** line, where possible, putting into practice all the keys you have learned so far.

```
Zoe went to the zoo to the see the zebra.      (7)
You must always cross at the zebra crossing.   (9)
Put your typing paper in at zero.              (6)
The lemonade was too fizzy.                    (5)
Go dancing at the Plaza tonight.               (6)
The rocket zoomed upwards to the sky.          (7)
The zinc ointment healed the wound.            (7)
Buy a pizza for tea today.                     (5)
You must all make a zealous effort.            (7)
His motorbike was a zippy machine.             (7)
```

Check your **speed**!

44

Introduction to number reaches

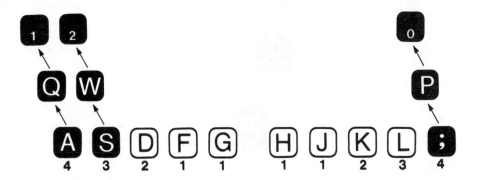

Although there is a figure 'one' on the top row of keys, it is easier **on a typewriter**, to use the letter 'l' for number one because your third finger of your right hand is already resting on this key. Instead of reaching with the little finger of the right hand **up** to the **left**, for the figure '0' on the top row of keys, the Capital Letter 'O' may be used.

The above instructions **do not** apply when **using a computer**, however. The following instructions must be followed for figures 'one' and 'nought': –

To strike any of the figures on the top row of keys, needs extra effort, because these figures require a longer reach by the fingers from the Home Keys. In the case of the number 1 – practise the reach with the fourth finger of the left hand from 'a' **up** to the **left** for the letter 'q' and then a further reach **up** to the **left** for the figure '1'. The movement you have just practised is 'aq1'. Having reached up for the number '1' return your finger to the resting position on the Home Key.

Type **two lines** of the following: –

```
aq1 aq1 aq1 aq1 aq1 aq1 aq1 aq1
aq1 aq1 aq1 aq1 aq1 aq1 aq1 aq1
```

With the fourth finger of the right hand, reach from ';' **up** to the **left** for the letter 'p' and then a further reach **up** to the **left** for the figure '0' then return your finger to the Home Key.

Type **two lines** of the following: –

```
;p0 ;p0 ;p0 ;p0 ;p0 ;p0 ;p0 ;p0
;p0 ;p0 ;p0 ;p0 ;p0 ;p0 ;p0 ;p0
```

Practise the reach with the third finger of the left hand from the 's' **up** to the **left** to the letter 'w' and then a further reach up to the figure '2'. The movement you have just practised is 'sw2'. Having reached up for the number '2' return your finger to the resting position on the Home Key.

Type **two lines** of the following: –

```
sw2 sw2 sw2 sw2 sw2 sw2 sw2 sw2
sw2 sw2 sw2 sw2 sw2 sw2 sw2 sw2
```

Bearing in mind the instructions given for the typing of number one and the figure '0' type **two lines** of the following sentences, but remember computer operators must always use the figure keys on the top row of the machine: –

```
The lll men canoed along the canal.
The lll men canoed along the canal.
There were 110 pages in the book.
There were 110 pages in the book.
```

Type **two lines of each** of the following: –

```
s2s s2s s2s s2s s2s s2s s2s s2s
I know 21 men who need 21 shirts.
There are 202 guests going to the wedding.
Meet me at 121, Church Street at 2.00 p.m.
```

New number reach

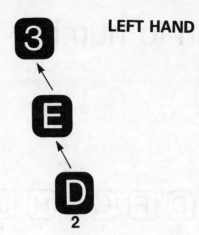

Practise the reach with the second finger of the left hand from 'd' **up** to the **left** to the letter 'e' and then a further reach up to the figure '3'. **Remember** now to return your finger to the Home Key before attempting this number reach again.

Type **two lines** of the following: –

```
de3 de3 de3 de3 de3 de3 de3 de3 de3
de3 de3 de3 de3 de3 de3 de3 de3 de3
```

Type **two lines** of **each** of the following: –

```
d3d d3d d3d d3d d3d d3d d3d d3d d3d
d3d d3d d3d d3d d3d d3d d3d d3d d3d
```

Type **two lines** of **each** of the following sentences: –

```
Julie was born on the 3rd May this year.
Julie was born on the 3rd May this year.

The Cricket Club had 33 members.
The Cricket Club had 33 members.

The shop will close at 3.00 p.m. today.
The shop will close at 3.00 p.m. today.

Only 333 people survived the earthquake.
Only 333 people survived the earthquake.

The number of my house is 123.
The number of my house is 123.

My friend lives at 103 Park Street, York.
My friend lives at 103 Park Street, York.
```

New number reach

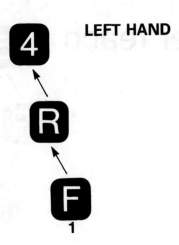

Practise the reach with the first finger of the left hand from 'f' **up** to the **left** for the figure '4'. **Remember** now to return your finger to the Home Key before attempting this number reach again.

Type **two lines** of the following: –

```
fr4 fr4 fr4 fr4 fr4 fr4 fr4 fr4
fr4 fr4 fr4 fr4 fr4 fr4 fr4 fr4
```

Type **two lines** of the following: –

```
f4f f4f f4f f4f f4f f4f f4f f4f
f4f f4f f4f f4f f4f f4f f4f f4f
```

Type **two lines** of **each** of the following sentences: –

```
The winning raffle ticket number was 404.
The winning raffle ticket number was 404.

Mary has taken 124 pictures of the gala.
Mary has taken 124 pictures of the gala.

There are 342 children in the Primary School.
There are 342 children in the Primary School.
```

New number reach

LEFT HAND

Practise the reach with the first finger of the left hand from 'f' **up** to the **right** this time, for the figure '5'. **Remember** now to return your finger to the Home Key before attempting this number reach again.

Type **two lines** of the following: —

```
f5f  f5f  f5f  f5f  f5f  f5f  f5f  f5f
f5f  f5f  f5f  f5f  f5f  f5f  f5f  f5f
```

Type **two lines** of **each** of the following sentences: —

```
Please take 51 chairs to the canteen.
Please take 51 chairs to the canteen.

Have you 25 spare pencils please?
Have you 25 spare pencils please?

I awoke at 5.00 a.m. today.
I awoke at 5.00 a.m. today.
```

Consolidation practice

LEFT HAND

Type **two lines** of **each** of the following, with the first finger of the left hand: —

```
f4f5f  f4f5f  f4f5f  f4f5f  f4f5f  f4f5f
f4f5f  f4f5f  f4f5f  f4f5f  f4f5f  f4f5f
```

Type **two lines** of **each** of the following sentences:

```
Bring me 45 pairs of socks from the warehouse.
The 14th and 15th June are the dates chosen.
The bell will ring in 45 seconds.
```

New number reach

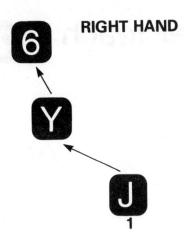

Practise the reach with the first finger of the right hand from 'j' **up** to the **left** – which is an extra long reach – to the figure '6'. **Remember** now to return your finger to the Home Key before attempting this number reach again.

Type **two lines** of the following: –

```
jy6 jy6 jy6 jy6 jy6 jy6 jy6 jy6 jy6
jy6 jy6 jy6 jy6 jy6 jy6 jy6 jy6 jy6
```

Type **two lines** of the following: –

```
j6j j6j j6j j6j j6j j6j j6j j6j j6j
j6j j6j j6j j6j j6j j6j j6j j6j j6j
```

Keep your **wrists up** to allow your fingers to make this extra long reach.

Type **two lines** of **each** of the following sentences: –

```
Can you count up to 66?
Can you count up to 66?

The salesman sold 106 anoraks to the shop.
The salesman sold 106 anoraks to the shop.

The number of his cycle frame was 6264656.
The number of his cycle frame was 6264656.
```

New number reach

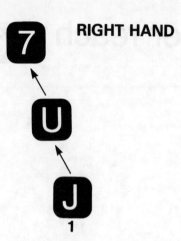

RIGHT HAND

Practise the reach with the first finger of the **right hand** from 'j' **up** to the **left** to the letter 'u' and then a further reach up to the figure '7'. Now return your finger to the Home Key before attempting this number reach again.

Type **two lines** of the following: –

```
ju7 ju7 ju7 ju7 ju7 ju7 ju7 ju7 ju7
ju7 ju7 ju7 ju7 ju7 ju7 ju7 ju7 ju7
```

Type **two lines** of the following: –

```
j7j j7j j7j j7j j7j j7j j7j j7j j7j
j7j j7j j7j j7j j7j j7j j7j j7j j7j
```

Type **two lines** of **each** of the following sentences: –

```
The order was delivered within 7 days.
The order was delivered within 7 days.

The price of the ticket was 70p.
The price of the ticket was 70p.

There are 7 girls in a netball team.
There are 7 girls in a netball team.
```

Consolidation practice

Type **two lines** of **each** of the following: –

```
ju6 ju7 ju6 ju7 ju6 ju7 ju6 ju7
ju6 ju7 ju6 ju7 ju6 ju7 ju6 ju7

j6j7j j6j7j j6j7j j6j7j j6j7j j6j7j
j6j7j j6j7j j6j7j j6j7j j6j7j j6j7j

Jane reached 67 metres in the event.
The 6th and 7th April are the dates needed.
Grandma is 76 years of age in July.
```

New number reach

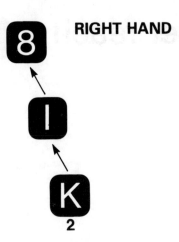 **RIGHT HAND**

Practise the reach with the second finger of the right hand from 'k' **up** to the **left** to the letter 'i' and then a further reach up to the figure '8'. Now return your finger to the Home Key before attempting this number reach again.

Type **two lines** of the following: –

```
ki8 ki8 ki8 ki8 ki8 ki8 ki8 ki8 ki8
ki8 ki8 ki8 ki8 ki8 ki8 ki8 ki8 ki8
```

Type **two lines** of the following: –

```
k8k k8k k8k k8k k8k k8k k8k k8k k8k
k8k k8k k8k k8k k8k k8k k8k k8k k8k
```

Type **two lines** of **each** of the following sentences: –

```
The disco starts at 8.00 p.m.
The disco starts at 8.00 p.m.

There are 800 girls in the school.
There are 800 girls in the school.

The number 8 bus goes to town.
The number 8 bus goes to town.

There were 8,000 spectators at the match.
There were 8,000 spectators at the match.

He was aged 28 years when he got married.
He was aged 28 years when he got married.
```

New number reach

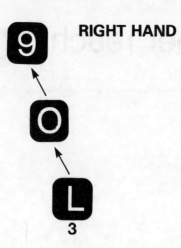

Practise the reach with the third finger of the right hand from 'l' **up** to the **left** to the letter 'o' and then a further reach up to the figure '9'. Now return your finger to the Home Key before attempting the number reach again.

The letter 'l' also acts as **Number One**.

Type **two lines** of the following: –

```
lo9 lo9 lo9 lo9 lo9 lo9 lo9 lo9 lo9
lo9 lo9 lo9 lo9 lo9 lo9 lo9 lo9 lo9
```

Type **two lines** of the following: –

```
191 191 191 191 191 191 191 191 191
191 191 191 191 191 191 191 191 191
```

Type **two lines** of **each** of the following sentences: –

```
The painting was done in the 19th Century.
The painting was done in the 19th Century.

The winner was a 19 years old student.
The winner was a 19 years old student.

All of the 90 seamen received bravery medals.
All of the 90 seamen received bravery medals.

Our holidays begin on the 19th August.
Our holidays begin on the 19th August.
```

New sign characters

To type the signs above the figures you need to use the Shift Keys – as you do when typing a Capital Letter.

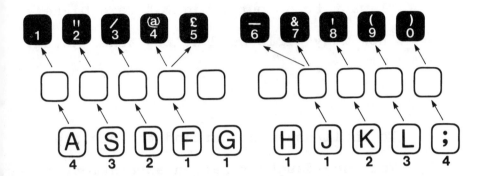

Where there are two characters on one key, the Shift Key must be used to type the top character on the key – to obtain the lower character, **no** Shift Key is necessary.

You will find that the Hyphen, right-closing Bracket, and Fraction Keys may appear in different positions on the keyboard, depending upon the make and model of the machine you are using.

Whichever make of machine is being used, always check the position of the keys required and these should be struck by the **fourth finger** of the right hand – with or without the use of the Shift Key.

There may, however, be one exception to the above statement. If the left-hand bracket, '(', appears on the top of the number '9' key, then the **third** finger of the right hand will be used.

Type **one line** of the following: –

```
s"s  s"s  s"s  s"s  s"s  s"s  s"s  s"s
d/d  d/d  d/d  d/d  d/d  d/d  d/d  d/d
f@f  f@f  f@f  f@f  f@f  f@f  f@f  f@f
f£f  f£f  f£f  f£f  f£f  f£f  f£f  f£f
j_j  j_j  j_j  j_j  j_j  j_j  j_j  j_j
k'k  k'k  k'k  k'k  k'k  k'k  k'k  k'k
l(l  l(l  l(l  l(l  l(l  l(l  l(l  l(l
;);  ;);  ;(;  ;);  ;);  ;);  ;);  ;);
```

Type the following sentences, putting into practice the use of the Shift Key for the signs above the number keys: –

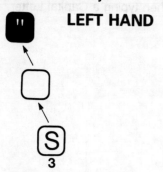

LEFT HAND

The Bishop said, "Please give generously to the Church Building Fund."

"I want to go out tonight," said Diane.

"How many girls need help?" asked Anita.

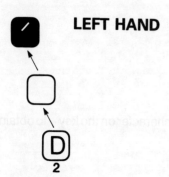

LEFT HAND

We shall/shall not attend the meeting.

Your son/daughter has an appointment today.

Do you require a red/black skirt?

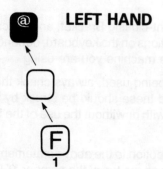

LEFT HAND

The order was for 2 dozen eggs @ 65p doz.

12 pencils @ 5p each and 10 rubbers @ 3p each are required immediately.

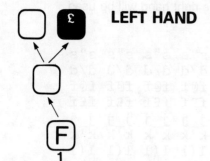

LEFT HAND

The cycles were sold for £80 each.

No space required after decimal point.

£2.50 plus £2.50 amounts to £5.00.

Each person was charged £2.00 entry fee.

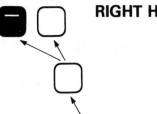

RIGHT HAND

The film is called "The Happiest Day
of my Life".

Headings and Titles are usually underlined.

DO NOT walk on the grass.

This is called the **Underscore** Key for underlining words, headings,
etc.

Type the following sentences: –

RIGHT HAND

James Brown & Co. are our paper suppliers.

Jones & Sons Ltd. are fish merchants.

The complaint was sent to Messrs. Buck & Clegg.

RIGHT HAND

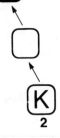

Peter's money was stolen from his pocket.

I must give Mary's dinner money to Jean.

The girl's shoes were not cleaned today.

There is no exclamation mark key on the typewriter, therefore we
have to combine two keys to give us this sign.

Whilst holding the Shift Key down, strike the apostrophe key which
is above the number 8. Release the Shift Key, **backspace once**
and strike the full stop key, which will come underneath the
apostrophe sign. This will give you an exclamation mark. (!)

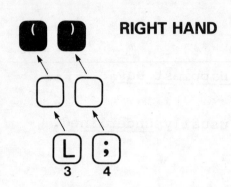

RIGHT HAND

Two brackets are usually typed when we use (a) (b) or (c).

The jumper(s) will be needed by Friday.

Some girls will stay behind (if necessary).

Consolidation practice

Type **two lines** of **each** of the following sentences: —

The number of the seat is 111 on the platform.
May is 20, Mary 22, John 24 and Jim 26.
Lucy has 13 blouses, 3 dresses and 3 jumpers.
On the 4th July, Alice will be 44 years old.
Our holidays are in 5 months, 5 weeks, 5 days.
The 6 brothers and 6 sisters are very happy.
£7.77 was charged for the 27 containers.
There were 88 villages destroyed in the fire.
Please allow only 990 passengers onto the ship.

Consolidation practice

Type **two lines** of **each** of the following sentences: —

"To which lesson have you just been?" asked the teacher.

The agreed price is less 2½% if paid within 14 days from <u>receipt of order</u>.

Peter's hat was found underneath the lockers in the boys' changing room.

I may/may not be home early today.

Messrs. Black & White are well known artists.

You may - if you are lucky - get a ticket.

There is no part-time job for you.

$\frac{1}{4} + \frac{1}{4} = \frac{1}{2}$. Add $\frac{1}{3} + \frac{2}{3}$. Take $\frac{5}{8}$ from $\frac{7}{8}$.

Consolidation of figure practice

Type the following addresses **fully blocked** —
which means that all lines **start** at the **same**
point.

Messrs. Smith & Jones,
18, Cross Street,
GORTON
Manchester.
M18 4RP

Monaghan Bros.,
'Rowan House',
Barker Hill,
MAIDENHEAD,
Berks.
SL6 2QL

Mrs. K. Rothwell,
18, Banbury Close,
PRESTON,
Lancs.
PR2 3UB

Hopwood & Wroe (Solicitors)
Universal House,
The Strand,
LYTHAM,
Lancs.
FY8 4PW

J. Dalahoyd (Decorator) Ltd.,
18, Alpine Drive,
DEVON.
TQ12 5NA

Miss E. Barlow,
c/o Rutherford House,
Lombard Street,
LONDON.
EC3V 98E

Cross Courts Sports Centre,
Wigan Old Road,
WIGAN.
WN2 1PX

The Lake View Hotel,
WINDEMERE,
Cumbria.
LA23 1LJ

Carriage return practice

Practise returning your carriage quickly, whilst at all times keeping your eyes on your book in readiness for the next line to be typed.

```
Humpty
Humpty Dumpty
Humpty Dumpty sat
Humpty Dumpty sat on
Humpty Dumpty sat on a
Humpty Dumpty sat on a wall.

Jack
Jack and
Jack and Jill
Jack and Jill went
Jack and Jill went up
Jack and Jill went up the
Jack and Jill went up the hill.

Three
Three blind
Three blind mice.
Three blind mice.  See
Three blind mice.  See how
Three blind mice.  See how they
Three blind mice.  See how they run.

Little
Little Jack
Little Jack Horner
Little Jack Horner sat
Little Jack Horner sat in
Little Jack Horner sat in a
Little Jack Horner sat in a corner.

I
I saw
I saw three
I saw three ships
I saw three ships go
I saw three ships go sailing
I saw three ships go sailing by.

Mary
Mary had
Mary had a
Mary had a little
Mary had a little lamb.
Mary had a little lamb.  Its
Mary had a little lamb.  Its fleece
Mary had a little lamb.  Its fleece was
Mary had a little lamb.  Its fleece was white
Mary had a little lamb.  Its fleece was white as
Mary had a little lamb.  Its fleece was white as snow.
```

Alphabetic speed sentences for general revision

A   Amanda and Anna arrived late last night at the Airport.

B   Barbara, Betty, Beryl, Beverley, Belinda, Brenda and Bridget are on the school netball team.

C   There is no chance of Clara coming to the concert without her clarinet.

D   The Doctor, together with the Dietician, visited David daily, in order to discuss his daily diet.

E   I hope every effort will be made to accommodate Kate and Betty.

F   Fred fired his weapon fast and furiously at five minutes past five.

G   The three grey geese on the green were grazing.

H   He hit him on the head with a hard hammer and he howled horribly.

I   The girl guides fried their eggs after lighting the camp fire.

J   Jennifer rejected help from Joyce to rejoin the 'Jolly Club'.

K   The cakes were baked by Kathy and taken to Cook in the kitchen.

L   The yellow light will be small but it would be useless to Leslie.

M   The commander jammed the communications until midnight.

N   The final begins at noon today and will end at nine tonight.

O   Those who own radios often have the volume too loud.

P   Peter Piper picked a peck of pickled pepper.

Q   The people queued quietly and moved quickly forward to receive their quota of tickets.

R   The aircraft carrier arrived at the correct time at Dover.

S   She sells sea shells on the sea shore on Saturdays and Sundays.

T   A letter of invitation was received by the pretty girl, to attend a party.

U   The court was upset about such ugly behaviour and quite suddenly adjourned until a later date.

V   Eva and Valerie never visited the very fine villa but loved to admire the view of it.

W   Worthwhile news is always worth waiting for.

X   The six extensions were exempt from examination which was expected.

Y   The cyclist displayed his ability today and won the prize money.

Z   The public were puzzled by the size of the zebras at the zoo.

Paragraphs

There are two types of paragraphs in use today. They are called **fully blocked** and **indented**.

FULLY BLOCKED Paragraphs

All paragraphs and lines following, are typed right against the left-hand margin until the completion of the paragraph. When the paragraph is completed and **before** beginning a new paragraph, you must **turn up twice** to allow **one clear line** space in between each paragraph. We also allow a clear line after a heading, as above this paragraph.

Type this paragraph and the one above, **twice** in the **fully blocked** style, putting into practice the instructions given.

INDENTED Paragraphs

The beginning of this paragraph has been **indented**, which means **set in** from the margin. In order to do this, you must tap five times on the Space Bar, before starting to type your paragraphs.

It is still necessary to **turn up twice** in between paragraphs in order to leave **one clear line** space, before starting the next paragraph.

Type this and the last two paragraphs **twice** in the **indented** style. When you have copied the above paragraphs, put these in your file for future reference.

When you are typing Fully Blocked Paragraphs in **double line spacing**, it is necessary to turn up a **double double** space (four lines) in between paragraphs, in order that you can see where one paragraph ends and a new one begins.

When typing Indented paragraphs in **double line spacing**, it is only necessary to turn up **one double** space between paragraphs, because you can see where the next paragraph begins by its indentation.

Type the following once in Fully Blocked style and once with Indented paragraphs. Both passages to be typed in **double line spacing**, using the correct spacing in between the paragraphs.

All typists should take a pride in their work. Accuracy is very important. An employer does not want to appoint a typist who cannot spell or correct their own mistakes and those of their executive. Always check your work thoroughly. If letters containing many errors are continually being sent out, this creates a bad impression of the firm in the business world. It is pleasing to receive well-displayed work, which has been carefully and accurately presented by the secretary.

A secretary must also be able to stand in for their executive if necessary, and may have to interview clients for them during their absence. No duplication of appointments in their diary must be allowed to occur. Reminders about appointments should be given to the executive each day by the secretary. The keeping of appointments at the stated time is very important. A personal secretary will probably have to arrange all flights and travel arrangements for their executive and, therefore, once again, accuracy is very important.

It is the secretary who plays an important part in the preparation of the room for Committee Meetings. The minutes of the meetings are taken down by the secretary, who must be attentive at all times. All important decisions, and action necessary, must be recorded and typed, and a copy of the minutes then sent to all the members of the Committee in due course.

Copying practice

Helen's Day Shopping

Helen's mother was a dressmaker who was always complaining that
the clothes today, especially in the teenage shops, were badly
made. Helen would argue defensively, stating that they were not
made to last as in the 'olden days', and that it was 'trendy' to
buy from certain shops.

One Saturday Helen went down to town. Her mother had given her
some money to spend on new clothes, but she had been told to shop
wisely and not to buy any clothes which had not been properly
'finished off'.

After looking at the window display of 'Trendy Gear' - her favour-
ite shop in town, Helen went inside. She liked this shop because
they allowed you to browse around without being continually dis-
turbed by shop assistants enquiring "Do you need any help, Madam?"
etc., which was what normally happened in the big Stores in town.

Sometimes, when Helen had visited the shop, the selection of
dresses had been very poor, but today she was lucky. The new
Summer stock had arrived the previous day so this time she was
spoilt for choice. Eventually after trying three or four dresses
on, she made her final decision. Yes, I will have the blue dress,
she thought. I can then buy some white shoes to match this and
my dresses at home.

The buying of the shoes should have been quite straight-forward,
but today she was having difficulty in getting the right size in
a modern style. Each shop she visited was unable to be of
assistance to her and they recommended her to try various shops
in the town. In the end Helen was getting more and more
frustrated. It being the summer time, the window displays of
the shoe shops were of predominantly white shoes yet she was
unable to purchase the shoes she had hoped for.

However, in the window of the last shop she visited, she saw a
style she liked, and although she was unable to obtain the shoes
in white in her size, the Manager was able to offer her the same
style of shoe in her size, in a beige colour. This satisfied
Helen very much so home she then went with her shoes and dress
to show her mother and await her criticisms, which were usually
"Oh dear! Those won't last five minutes" or "I could have made
better myself," or "You're not going out in that are you?"

After arriving home and listening to the usual comments, Helen
proudly put her new shoes and dress in her wardrobe and looked
forward to wearing them at her friend's 18th Birthday Party that
evening.

Copying practice
in double line spacing

BADMINTON

Badminton has become a very popular game. The building
of many new sports halls throughout the country, together with
television coverage of International events, has high-lighted
this sport.

Many schools have their own facilities and most towns
have invested in Sports Centres. More and more people nowadays
are health and exercise conscious and have taken up this sport
at a late stage in their lives. They are able to do this with
great enjoyment and can play the sport to the best of their
ability until quite advanced in years.

If children take the opportunity of starting badminton
at an early age, they usually become very good players. They
are quite often selected to represent their town team and
perhaps their County. Selection is usually then made from
County Players to represent England. To be chosen to represent
England is a great honour and offers the opportunity of
travelling to various countries all over the world.

Dedication and practice is necessary in all forms of sport.
Without these, a good standard cannot be achieved or sustained.
The same can also be said of typewriting!

PREPARING FOR HOLIDAYS

In order to make your holiday successful it is important that good and careful planning has taken place. This is especially so if you are contemplating a camping holiday.

A camping holiday is only going to be as comfortable as you are prepared to make it. Long lists with reminders about this and that have to be started in advance. One of the lists would be for food in order that the buying and preparation of this is not left to the last minute. Another list would be of the camping equipment, plus all the utensils, not forgetting the most important thing, 'the tin opener'!

If you are travelling to an area which is very popular, and has limited camping sites, an early booking is recommended in order to be sure of securing a place.

A camping holiday can be a most relaxing holiday. No clock-watching is necessary. A person can come and go as he or she pleases and various sites and areas may be visited throughout a fortnight's holiday.

To make the holiday a real success, it is necessary to have good weather, which cannot be guaranteed or planned in advance in England. It is only if you go abroad that you can, more or less, be guaranteed good weather. Whichever holiday you decide to take, it is the preparation which is important in making it a success.